Bipolar Disorder and Depression

TOWNSHIP OF UNION
FREE PUBLIC LIBRARY

SUSAN DUDLEY GOLD

*Expert Reviews by Linda Zamvil, M.D.;
Robert L. Johnson, M.D., FAAP; and
James E. Aikens, Ph.D.*

Enslow Publishers, Inc.

40 Industrial Road	PO Box 38
Box 398	Aldershot
Berkeley Heights, NJ 07922	Hants GU12 6BP
USA	UK

http://www.enslow.com

Dedicated to my mother

Acknowledgments
With thanks to:
Linda Zamvil, M.D., Instructor in Psychiatry, Harvard Medical School, and Clinical Associate, Massachusetts General Hospital, for her advice and review of this book, her enthusiastic support of this project, and her invaluable assistance in contacting sources.
Jennifer Ellis and her family, the Boisvert family, Rachel, and Erin and her family, who shared their stories to make this book possible.
Karen Neale Leary, for her much-appreciated help in contacting sources for this book and the excellent resources she provided.
Esther Dudley, for her valuable help in contacting sources for this book.

Library of Congress Cataloging-in-Publication Data
Gold, Susan Dudley.
    Bipolar disorder and depression / Susan Dudley Gold; expert review by Linda Zamvil.
        p. cm. —— (Health watch)
    Includes bibliographical references and index.
    Summary: Discusses the symptoms, diagnosis, cause, and treatment of bipolar disorder, also known as manic depression, a mental illness that causes a person's moods to swing from happy and energized to extremely sad.
    ISBN 0-7660-1654-4 (hardcover)
    1. Manic-depressive illness—Juvenile literature. 2. Depression, Mental—Juvenile literature. [1. Manic-depressive illness. 2. Diseases. 2. Depression, Mental. 3. Mental illness.] I. Zamvil, Linda. II. Title. III. Health watch (Berkeley Heights, N.J.)
    RC516.G65 2000
    616.89'5—dc21
                            00-008384
Printed in the United States of America

10 9 8 7 6 5 4 3 2

To Our Readers: We have done our best to make sure all Internet addresses in this book were active and appropriate when we went to press. However, the author and the publisher have no control over and assume no liability for the material available on those Internet sites or on other Web sites they may link to. Any comments or suggestions can be sent by e-mail to comments@enslow.com or to the address on the back cover.

Illustration and Photo Credits:
© PhotoDisc, Inc.: pp. 1, 9, 10, 12, 15, 24, 28, 31, 38; courtesy of the Ellis Family: pp. 4, 6; © Digital Stock, Corbis Corp.: pp. 16, 27; © Jill K. Gregory, p. 19; courtesy of the Boisvert Family, pp. 21, 40.

Cover Illustrations:
Large photo, © PhotoDisc, Inc.; illustration, © Jill K. Gregory; inset, courtesy of the Ellis Family.

Contents

"Life is much easier. I feel my life is finally back on track and I'm ready to go."—Jennifer Ellis

Chapter 1

Highs, Lows, and Despair

A week before her fourteenth birthday, Jennifer Ellis thought she could fly—or become a movie star. She believed she could do anything and everything. "I kept running and hitting my head into the wall," she said. "I didn't sleep for a week. I kept hearing things. I talked to chairs. I was off the wall."

Jennifer has **bipolar disorder**, also known as **manic depression**, a mental illness that causes a person's moods to swing from very happy and energized (a high known as **mania**) to extremely sad (a low, or **depression**).

Bipolar disorder is a **mood disorder**, a condition that affects a person's mood. Mood disorders can have a dramatic effect on people's lives.

When Jennifer was manic, she talked constantly, so fast that no one could understand what she was saying. Her thoughts raced from one bizarre plan to another. She breathed rapidly, like someone who had just run a mile, but she wasn't at all tired. "I had all this energy," she said.

Other times, Jennifer's mood shifted to the opposite extreme. When she was only six years old, Jennifer tried to jump out a window because she was so depressed. After that attempt to end her life failed, she spent hours planning ways to kill herself. She remembers living under a cloud of sadness for years.

Jennifer Ellis at about three years old.

Rachel's Story

Some people experience depression only, without mania. Rachel was twenty and in her senior year of nursing school when a heavy sadness swept over her. In the morning her alarm clock rang every ten minutes, but she couldn't get out of bed. She missed classes, cried all the time, and feared the future. When she went to the school's doctor for help, he gave her a few **tranquilizers** to calm her and told her nothing was wrong with her. A tranquilizer is medicine that makes people feel less anxious.

"Somehow I muddled through," she said, recalling that difficult time. The sadness retreated to the background as she graduated from school and became engaged to be married. But it soon returned, haunting her for years.

"Minor problems seemed huge," Rachel said. "I walked

around with a knot in my stomach all the time. I couldn't concentrate. My whole body slowed down." At times she felt so sad that she couldn't eat. During one six-month period, she lost twenty pounds without trying. Other times, she became so anxious that she ate constantly and put on weight.

By the time Rachel turned thirty, she was severely depressed. She had three children under the age of five and had to push herself to get through each day. During her darkest times, she could barely do the grocery shopping. "Meeting people and making small talk seemed almost impossible," she said. When she returned from the market, she agonized over what she had said and what people thought of her.

Each day, Rachel forced herself out of bed, dressed and fed the children, and took them outside to play. Her neighbors laughed and chatted as their children played in the sun. Rachel felt nothing but gloom. "Nothing was enjoyable," she said.

She considered killing herself to end her misery. But she knew her children would be left motherless if she committed suicide. Perhaps, she thought, she should kill everyone in the family: her children, her husband, and herself. Then no one would be trapped in the darkness that surrounded their home.

Rachel shuddered at the awful thoughts that seemed to take over her mind. She was terrified that she could think such things. Guilt and a feeling of worthlessness consumed her, and she cried for hours.

With the help of medication and counseling, both Jennifer and Rachel learned how to cope with their disorders.

Chapter 2

What Are Mood Disorders?

M ood disorders affect millions of Americans. Researchers believe these disorders are linked to a chemical imbalance in the brain.

The two most common mood disorders are bipolar disorder (so named because it has two extremes of behavior) and depression (also called **unipolar depression**, because it has just one extreme of behavior). People with bipolar disorder (manic depression) have both highs (mania) and lows (depression) that last for at least a week. Those with depression are sad, anxious, tired, and listless most of the time. They have problems with sleep, either sleeping too much or too little. They may overeat or have no interest in food. The future seems bleak and hopeless to depressed people. They see no end to their sadness.

There is no cure for either bipolar disorder or depression, but both disorders can be treated with medication or counseling or both. For some the **symptoms** disappear completely after treatment.

Two to three million American adults have been diagnosed with bipolar disorder. Many more probably have the disease and don't know it. The National Institute of Mental Health estimates that one in every one hundred people will develop the disorder. It strikes women and men equally and people of all

President Abraham Lincoln is one of many distinguished leaders thought to have had a mood disorder; in his case, it was depression.

races. Signs of bipolar disorder usually first appear in a person's late teens or early twenties, but symptoms can occur in children and in older people as well.

Unipolar depression is even more common, affecting 4.4 percent of the United States population, a total of 9.4 million Americans. Women are two to three times more likely to have depression than men. Most people first experience depression in their mid-twenties, but children, the elderly, and everyone in between can have the disorder.

Both disorders are life-threatening, **chronic illnesses**. Twenty percent of people with bipolar disorder who have not been treated or have not found a successful treatment commit suicide. Fifteen percent of those with depression kill themselves, and many more attempt to end their lives.

During the manic phase of bipolar disorder, people injure themselves and sometimes others by doing dangerous acts. That is why it is so important for people with bipolar disorder and depression to seek treatment.

Mood disorders seem to be linked to creativity. According to writer and psychiatrist Kay Jamison, an expert on mood disorders who herself has bipolar disorder, artists are ten to forty times more likely to have the disorder than members of the general public. Other researchers have noted the high number of writers, composers, and political leaders who were thought to have had mood disorders. Artist Vincent van Gogh, poet Sylvia Plath, writer Ernest Hemingway, President Abraham Lincoln, and British Prime Minister Winston Churchill are among the noted figures who had depression or bipolar disorder. Jennifer Ellis, whom we met in Chapter 1, is an accomplished dancer, writes poetry, and participates in honors classes in English and history.

People with depression or bipolar disorder are also more likely than others to abuse drugs or alcohol. One study showed that 61 percent of those diagnosed with bipolar disorder had

People with mood disorders are at risk for drug and alcohol abuse.

substance abuse problems. It is not clear whether people with mood disorders drink or take drugs to try to deal with their illness or whether the chemical imbalance that causes their disorder is also linked to substance abuse.

Types of Bipolar Disorder

There are two types of bipolar disorder: **Bipolar I** and **Bipolar II**. People with Bipolar I go through cycles of major depression and mania. Bipolar II (the form that Jennifer has) is similar to Bipolar I, except that people have **hypomanic** episodes, a milder form of mania. People in a manic or hypomanic state feel euphoric—very happy and full of energy. They may be especially creative during this time, writing poetry, thinking of different ways of doing things, starting new projects.

Feelings during mania are intense. Psychiatrist Kay Jamison, in her book on bipolar disorder, *An Unquiet Mind*, wrote that as a result of bipolar disorder, "I have felt more things, more deeply; had more experiences, more intensely; loved more, and been more loved; laughed more often, for having cried more often; appreciated more the springs, for all the winters."

But as the episode continues, manic or hypomanic people may not be able to carry out their creative ideas. Their high-energy moods may lead them to jump from task to task. Ideas may race through their heads so fast that they can't focus (a state called **thought racing**). They may not be able to sit still long enough to finish a project.

"It feels like you can do anything, but it also feels like you can't control anything you do," Jennifer Ellis said,

People in a manic phase sometimes have difficulty controlling their temper.

describing the times when she is manic. The loss of control is frightening. "I was floating around in the galaxy," Jennifer said, "and I wanted to come back, but I couldn't."

People who are in a manic phase may also become enraged if they can't do what they want to do or if problems arise. They can't judge what's important. Many overreact to little things, act without thinking, and don't believe their behavior is bizarre or out of line at the time. Erin is an eleven-year-old girl who, like Jennifer, has bipolar disorder. During manic episodes she said she exploded into temper tantrums for no reason.

"Everything was a crisis," she said. "I could be perfectly fine, and then my mom might say something I didn't like, and I'd have a temper tantrum." During one episode she picked up a broom and hit her mother on the head with it.

Mania may cause people to swerve out of control. Some people go on spending sprees, buying items they don't need or want. Others quit jobs or get fired because of their bizarre behavior.

Rachel's brother, who has bipolar disorder, believed he

could be elected mayor of the city where he lived, despite the fact that he was unemployed and had no political experience or qualifications for the job.

Although some people are able to function quite well when they are hypomanic or at the beginning of a manic phase, the slide into depression puts an end to all that. The contrast between the high of mania and the low of depression can be especially hard to endure. "Everything's down," Jennifer said of the times when she was depressed. "I'd rather stay in bed and sleep. I'd forget about eating and think about suicide all the time."

In between episodes many people with bipolar disorder live normally, with few severe mood shifts. There doesn't seem to be any regular cycle of mania and depression. Some people have long periods of depression followed by a manic episode months, or sometimes years, later. Others have lengthy manias and brief depressions. For some, the cold, dark days of winter bring on depression, a condition called **seasonal affective disorder**.

Some people switch quickly from mania to depression with no break in between. These people are called **rapid cyclers** and are the hardest to treat. They have at least four episodes of mania or depression or both over the course of a year.

Other people have **mixed bipolar disorder**, a combination of mania and depression. These people have symptoms of both phases at the same time. They can be irritable and feel sad but still have lots of energy, for example. One doctor compares mixed bipolar disorder to "driving with one foot on the brake and the other foot on the accelerator at the same time."

Those with **cyclothymic disorder** have a mild form of bipolar disorder. People with this type feel low and then high, but the highs and lows aren't as extreme as in bipolar disorder. The problem is that the constant change in mood makes it hard for people with untreated cyclothymic disorder to plan their lives. They never know how they will feel on a particular day.

Types of Depression

Everyone feels depressed now and then. It is natural to feel sad when a loved one dies or a problem at school or work arises. But a person who is sad most of the day, day in and day out for two weeks or more, probably is suffering from depression.

Depression affects every part of a person's life, from waking up in the morning to eating to relating to other people. The symptoms of unipolar depression are the same as those of the depression period of bipolar disorder. The illness saps people's strength and makes them feel worthless and helpless. Even though Rachel had done well in school and had worked as a nurse, she felt she didn't have the energy or the ability to care for her children. "I could hardly take care of myself," she recalled.

Life seems hopeless to depressed people. They often believe that the only way to escape from the gloom is to kill themselves. In fact, depression is the most common cause of suicide. People suffering from severe depression may not be able to work, eat, put on their clothes, or wash themselves. In addition to the human toll, depression costs the nation $44 billion in treatment fees and in jobs left undone when depressed people can't work.

There are two kinds of unipolar depression: typical (or **melancholic**) and atypical. Those with **typical depression** lose weight, are always tired, and may wake up in the middle of the night or early in the morning and not be able to get back to sleep. People with this type of depression feel the worst in the morning. They have no interest in life, feel no joy, and have no appetite. They also may feel guilty and restless.

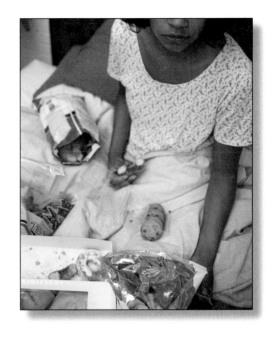

Some people overeat when they are depressed. Others don't eat enough.

Those with **atypical depression** overeat and sleep too much (sometimes as much as fifteen to twenty hours a day). They may feel happy for a moment, but it passes quickly. Their arms and legs feel like lead. A slight disagreement or misunderstanding can cause them to think other people are rejecting them. In severe depression and severe mania, people may become catatonic, or unable to move.

A milder form of depression, called **dysthymia**, affects 6.4 percent of the U.S. population. People who suffer from this disorder feel sad almost all the time for years at a time. They are able to get by each day but don't have

A person having a psychotic episode can think he or she can do dangerous things without harm.

much energy, lack self-confidence, and have trouble concentrating. Many people with dysthymia think it is normal to be sad all the time. These people do not know they have a disorder.

Seeing Things That Are Not There

People with mood disorders sometimes **hallucinate**, which means they hear voices or see images that are not really there. These hallucinations can appear during both mania and depression. In some cases the voices may tell people to kill themselves or to hurt others. During mania, people also may have **delusions of grandeur**, beliefs that they can do impossible acts. When Jennifer Ellis was manic, she thought she could fly like a bird. She also heard voices during one episode. Some people have **paranoid delusions** that make them think that others want to hurt or kill them.

People who have hallucinations and delusions are said to be **psychotic**, which means that they no longer know what's real. Jennifer felt so out of touch with reality during one manic episode that she wasn't sure she existed. "I had to touch myself to make sure I was still there," she said.

Psychotic episodes can also be very dangerous. Jim Boisvert is a young man who, like Jennifer and Erin, has been diagnosed with bipolar disorder. When he was fifteen, during a manic episode, Jim became convinced that he could walk along an ice-encrusted embankment. He fell down the steep incline, shattering his leg. Rescue workers had to drive an ambulance along railroad tracks at the bottom of the hill to reach the injured boy. "I didn't think I could hurt myself," Jim told his mother afterward.

Chapter 3

How the Brain Works

T he brain controls everything a person does, thinks, feels, believes, remembers, smells, sees, and hears. Think of the brain as the body's general manager. Sitting in the body's "control booth," the brain receives information from the members of the team—the ears, the eyes, the nose, the skin, and other parts of the body—by way of nerves. As the reports filter in, the brain studies the material and draws up a game plan. Then the brain sends out orders to the body on how it should respond to the information that has been gathered.

The messages between the brain and the rest of the body are carried along a complex network made up of billions of nerve cells. These cells, called **neurons**, pass along messages to and from the brain by a series of electrical charges and chemicals.

When a neuron is stimulated, it gives off an electrical charge. The electrical charge causes a chemical called a

neurotransmitter to be released. The chemical in turn stimulates the neuron next in line, which gives off another electrical charge and releases more chemicals. In this way the message is carried along the chain of neurons either to the brain or from the brain to the rest of the body. A

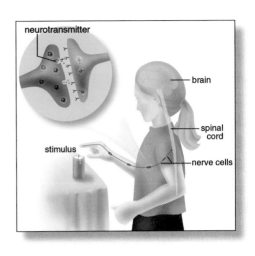

An artist's drawing of how the brain sends messages.

message can travel to the brain and back very rapidly, as fast as 660 feet (200 meters) per second.

Each neurotransmitter carries its own message. The neurotransmitter **serotonin** has been linked to sleep and emotions. **Dopamine** prevents muscles from shaking or moving too much; it also can cause feelings of euphoria or extreme happiness (feeling high). **Epinephrine**, which speeds up the heart rate and increases blood pressure, is released during periods of fear and anxiety, while **norepinephrine** is linked to happiness and sadness.

Suppose, for example, a loud noise stimulates the neurons in a person's brain. The neurons release the neurotransmitter epinephrine, which sends a ripple of fear through the person. A sad movie or the tantalizing smells of Thanksgiving dinner may cause the neurons to send other types of messages—of sadness or pleasure—to the brain. The intense feeling is usually brief. Once the neurotransmitter has done its job, it is quickly absorbed by the neuron that released it.

Causes of Mood Disorders

Most scientists now agree that bipolar disorder and depression are linked to a chemical imbalance in the brain. The chemicals that control sleep, fear, anxiety, and other functions may be affected.

No one knows for sure exactly which chemicals are to blame or why and how they are out of balance. Studies suggest that the chemical imbalance can be triggered by a number of factors. An injury or illness, the death of a loved one, a lack of sleep, a major change in one's life, or worry can upset the body's delicate balance. Such an event can act like a wrench that is dropped into a running engine. Someone who has bipolar disorder may become manic or depressed as a result. A person who is depressed may become even less able to cope than usual.

The change of seasons triggers Jim Boisvert's disorder. At the first signs of winter, he becomes pale and agitated. The shock of breaking his leg led to even more bizarre behavior. He began to sleepwalk and have nightmares. One night his mother awoke to find Jim standing over her with a hatchet, screaming in terror.

Kay Jamison began hallucinating after the stress of working long hours and sleeping little. Rachel's darkest depressions came just before or just after major events in her life—her graduation from nursing school, the birth of her children, a move to a new city. Sometimes, however, a depression or a mania appears for no apparent reason.

Some researchers believe mood disorders may be caused or made worse by events in childhood. A child who has been abused may feel helpless and angry. A parent's death may cause a child to feel overwhelming sadness. If children aren't taught to deal with these feelings, they may not be able to cope effectively with life or may think badly of themselves. This may put them at risk for developing mood disorders.

Hereditary Factors

We all inherit **genes** from our parents. These tiny units in our cells carry instructions that determine our traits, such as body build and eye color. We say we inherit these traits from our parents. Researchers believe the tendency to develop mood disorders may be included in the genes that are passed down from parents to children. The disorders often run in families.

People who have close relatives with mood disorders are much more likely to have a mood disorder themselves. The Boisvert family has three sons and a grandson who have been diagnosed with bipolar disorder. Rachel's brother has bipolar disorder, and her father and

Jim Boisvert, whose family has several members with bipolar disorder.

her aunt suffered from unipolar depression. Both Jennifer Ellis and Erin have family members who have been diagnosed as depressed or who show symptoms of mood disorders.

Depression and bipolar disorder also can affect people with no family history of mood disorders. Researchers believe that mood disorders may be caused by many different factors. One study showed a possible link between exposure to flu in pregnant mothers and mood disorders in their children. Some researchers think a number of factors that impair the development of the brain—disease, viruses, accidents, or other causes—may be linked to mood disorders. Scientists continue to search for the answers as they study the brain and its development.

Chapter 4

Diagnosis

Diagnosing mood disorders can be difficult. There is no one test that confirms a person has depression or bipolar disorder. Doctors first perform a physical examination to make sure other illnesses aren't causing the symptoms. Cancer or thyroid problems, for example, can cause people to have trouble sleeping, have no appetite, or feel tired—the same symptoms as depression. Bipolar disorder may be confused with several other mental disorders, including **attention deficit hyperactivity disorder** and **schizophrenia**. It is often hard to tell whether a person is suffering from unipolar depression or the depression of bipolar disorder.

After a physical examination, the next step may involve a series of oral or written tests designed to reveal the patient's thoughts and feelings. These tests can be conducted at a **therapist**'s office, at a hospital or a mental health center, or in a doctor's office.

The Children's Depression Inventory asks children about their symptoms. These tests are especially helpful in detecting depression in children who can't express their feelings well. Other tests ask parents and teachers to report on a child's behavior at home and in school. A tester may ask a child who can't yet read to complete various sentences, tell a story, or draw pictures. Testers may observe how children behave in certain circumstances as a way to detect whether they have mood disorders.

A boy answers questions on a test designed to reveal his thoughts and feelings.

At the mental health center where Jennifer was taken during a manic episode, she took one test in which she described a series of ink blots. During another test the center's staff gave Jennifer blocks with pictures on them and asked her to put them in order. A third test required her to place colored blocks to match a certain pattern. Jennifer's performances on these tests provided clues about how her brain was working and how she was thinking and feeling.

Diagnosing Depression

Doctors who suspect depression look for the following symptoms in a patient:

- Feeling depressed or sad for most of the time every day for at least two weeks.

- Having no interest in usual activities.
- Losing or gaining weight for no reason.
- Sleeping more than ten hours a day or having trouble sleeping.
- Feeling slowed down or restless.
- Having little energy; feeling tired all the time.
- Feeling guilty or worthless.
- Having trouble concentrating.
- Thinking often of death or suicide.

Depression is suspected if a person has at least five of these symptoms. People with depression may also feel helpless, hopeless, or anxious.

Diagnosing Bipolar Disorder

A person who is having a manic episode will feel excessively happy for at least a week. Some people, especially children, may be irritable instead of happy. At least three or four of the following symptoms also are present in people with mania:
- Feeling that the person can do anything.
- Not needing much sleep (two to three hours a night).
- Talking constantly at a rapid pace.
- Having thought racing or **flight of ideas** (when a person's thoughts or speech switches rapidly from one thing to another).
- Being easily distracted.
- Being much more active than usual; involved in all kinds of projects at work or home.

- Doing things to excess—going on a shopping spree, giving away all of one's money, or performing other actions that are dangerous or harmful to the person.

People having manic episodes may repeatedly rhyme words or make puns, laugh at inappropriate times, or be overly religious. They may have hallucinations or be unusually creative. Some move quickly and are so full of energy that others can't keep up with them. They may go into a rage or become exhausted from the constant activity and from lack of sleep and food.

At Last, a Name

When Jim Boisvert's mother, Brenda, learned her son had bipolar disorder, she felt relief. "It has a name," she recalled thinking. "Now I know what it is. Teach me to deal with it."

Erin's mother, who takes medication herself for depression, had a similar reaction. "I knew something was chemically wrong with her, and I knew there must be something she could take to make her feel better."

The person with the disorder, however, may feel differently about the diagnosis. Erin remembers being outraged when a doctor told her she had bipolar disorder. "I said, 'I'm not sick. I'm a normal kid. I've got no problems.' "

Mrs. Boisvert said Jim rebelled against a diagnosis that set him apart from others. "His reaction was, 'I'm different. There's something wrong with me. I won't be that way.' " But as treatment began to help him, Jim accepted

During a manic phase, people have a tremendous amount of energy.

the fact that he had bipolar disorder and that he could deal with it. "He decided he had a choice," Mrs. Boisvert said. He could take medication or he could continue being out of control. Jim chose to take medication. "He's done very well," his mother said.

Chapter 5

Treatment

People often don't know they have a mood disorder. Even if they suspect something is wrong, people with a mood disorder may deny they have an illness.

People in a manic phase rarely seek help on their own because they feel so wonderful. They don't believe anything is wrong.

People with depression may not have enough energy to seek help. "Depression eliminates your self-confidence," said Rachel. "You just can't push yourself." Others with a mood disorder mistakenly think they should be able to overcome their problems on their own or are ashamed to admit that they might need help. Researchers believe that

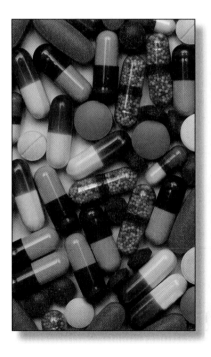

Many types of medications are available to treat mood disorders.

fewer than one-third of people who suffer from depression seek treatment. Kay Jamison estimates only 27 percent of those with bipolar disorder get treated for the disorder.

Medications

Although there is no known cure, there are many treatments for mood disorders. Researchers believe certain medications help balance the brain chemicals linked to mood disorders. They don't know exactly how the medications work, but they have seen good results. About 70 to 80 percent of those who have depression improve when treated with medication. Many of these medications, however, take several weeks or longer to work and have serious **side effects**, which are discussed later in this chapter. Some people can't take medications at all because the side effects are too severe. For others, scientists have not yet found a treatment that will help them.

Medications for mood disorders can be prescribed only by a psychiatrist or other doctor. The doctor helps select the drug best suited to the patient, adjusts the dosage if necessary, and keeps a watchful eye on side effects that can be dangerous. **Lithium**, a medication used for bipolar disorder, reduces symptoms for up to 70 percent of those who take it.

Antidepressants (medications that lift a patient's mood) are among the most useful for depression today. A new type of antidepressant, the **selective serotonin reuptake inhibitors (SSRIs)**, works very well for many people with depression and other mental disorders. Prozac and Zoloft are among the better known SSRIs available today. SSRIs block the neurons from reabsorbing serotonin, a neuro-transmitter that has been found to affect mood. Several studies have linked depression to low levels of serotonin. SSRIs increase the serotonin levels of patients who take the medication. Rachel, who takes an SSRI for her depression, compares the introduction of SSRIs to the discovery of penicillin for infection. "They're miracle drugs for people with mental illness," she said of SSRIs.

Monoamine oxidase inhibitors (MAOIs) are another form of depression medication that helps some people. MAOIs work best for those with atypical depression. Two common MAOIs are Nardil and Parnate. MAOIs also affect the chemicals in the brain. These medications block the destruction of serotonin and norepinephrine. Scientists don't know exactly how or why MAOIs work.

A number of medications are used to treat bipolar disorder. The most commonly used medication, lithium, was first prescribed for the disorder in the 1950s. It is a naturally occurring salt that reduces mood swings. For most people with bipolar disorder, lithium helps prevent both mania and depression. It is also used to treat patients who are having a manic episode.

Some people with bipolar disorder get help from **anti-seizure medications** (drugs that prevent seizures or brain spasms). Some of these are Depakote and Depakene, Neurontin, and Tegretol. Other people are helped by drugs that make people less anxious. Antidepressants can help reduce depression in bipolar disorder, but if used alone they can trigger mania or make the depression worse. Antipsychotic medications such as Trilafon, Risperdal, and Seroquel, among others, help prevent hallucinations. They

Frequent blood tests are necessary to make sure medications are not harming the body.

are often used with lithium or another mood stabilizer to prevent manic episodes.

Often people with depression or bipolar disorder use two or more medications to get the best results. Jennifer Ellis takes lithium, Trilafon (an antipsychotic medication), and Wellbutrin (an antidepressant) to treat her disorder. She also takes Cogentin (normally used for Parkinson's disease, a brain disorder that causes the body to tremble) to help overcome side effects from the other medications.

Even though medications have proven helpful for mood disorders, many people refuse to take them. When she first began medication treatment, Erin took the pills out of her mouth and hid them. "I didn't want to believe something was wrong with me," she said. Kay Jamison is an expert on mood disorders, but even she stopped taking her medication several times.

Once they begin to feel better, many patients decide they no longer need medication. Without the drugs, they spiral into a mania or dive into a new depression. That is why it is important for patients to consult their doctor before they stop using a drug prescribed for them. With their doctor's guidance, some people with mood disorders can stop taking medication after a year or more without symptoms. The majority, however, need to take medication for years, sometimes for the rest of their lives. Just as people with diabetes rely on insulin to keep them healthy, many with mood disorders need medication to stay well.

Psychotherapy

In addition to medication, **psychotherapy** can help people who have mood disorders. During psychotherapy a patient talks with a therapist who helps him or her deal with problems. Often this means learning how to change behavior or how to alter ways of thinking about life. Therapy can help people learn how to get along better with others and work out their anger and grief. Because so many people don't want to take medication, therapists also can work with patients to accept the need for medication.

Talking with a therapist helps Rachel understand her illness and keep on track. "It helps me understand myself when I get so jumbled up, I can't think clearly," she said of her monthly visits.

With the help of her therapist, Erin learned to use words to express her feelings instead of temper tantrums. When Jennifer Ellis had a bad manic episode, she spent more than a week at a mental health center. There she received medication, talked with therapists, and participated in a group for people with mood disorders. While at the center, she learned how to talk about her problems and to deal with her illness.

People who use both types of treatment—medication and psychotherapy—seem to do better than those on one treatment alone. Jamison wrote in her book *An Unquiet Mind* that she needed both kinds of treatment to get well: "No pill can help me deal with the problem of not wanting to take pills. No psychotherapy alone can prevent my manias and depressions."

Other Treatments

Electroconvulsive therapy (ECT) has helped some people with mood disorders. Once called "electroshock treatment," ECT doesn't shock patients but rather causes them to have seizures (or brain spasms). In the past some doctors overused ECT or used it incorrectly. Because of those early abuses of ECT, the treatment is now used only as a last resort when medication or therapy doesn't work. It is also performed when a patient threatens to commit suicide and can't wait for medication to take effect.

A person receiving ECT is first given anesthesia, a medication to prevent pain. Electrodes are attached to the head, and a small electrical current is passed through the brain. This causes the person to have a seizure. A patient usually goes through six to twelve sessions over a two- to five-week period.

In one study, 80 percent of depressed patients receiving ECT improved. The treatment also has been shown to help reduce manic episodes in those with bipolar disorder. Researchers don't know for sure why ECT works, but they believe the electric current may affect the brain chemistry in some beneficial way.

The National Institutes of Health is funding a study to test whether St. John's wort, a popular herbal remedy, will work to ease depression. Studies conducted in Europe showed that the herb helped some patients who had mild to moderate depression. The European studies, however, lacked the strict controls of the NIH project. Until the study results are in, NIH experts caution against substituting the herb for medications already proven effective in treating depression.

Several other methods have helped people with mood disorders cope with their illness. These are used in addition to medication or other treatment. Patients often are asked to keep mood charts. Each day they record on the chart how they are feeling on a scale of 1 to 100 (with 1 being "the worst I've felt" and 100 being "the best I've felt"). If the chart shows severe mood shifts, they may need to change their medication or increase the dose.

Support groups offer people the chance to meet with others who have similar problems. Together they learn more about their illness and share ways of dealing with it. Exercise helps lift the mood of those who are mildly depressed. It can also improve the appetite, reduce stress, and help people sleep better. Eating well-balanced, healthy meals also has been shown to be beneficial.

Side Effects

Treatments can be very effective in controlling mood disorders. Some medications, however, have side effects such as nausea, headaches, constipation, and other problems. Usually the side effects go away after the first few weeks. Sometimes the side effects are so bad that a person cannot continue to take a certain medication. When that happens, the doctor may prescribe a different medication or another kind of treatment.

Rachel tried three different medications before she found one with side effects she could tolerate. One type of medication gave her headaches and made her tired and weak. Another caused painful muscle spasms. Antidepressants can make a person's mouth feel dry, make it hard to urinate or have bowel movements, or cause fainting. They can also cause mania in people with bipolar disorder.

People taking MAOIs must watch carefully what they eat. Certain medications and foods such as cheese, yogurt, ripe bananas, and ham should be avoided while taking MAOIs.

Jennifer Ellis became severely constipated after taking lithium. The medication also made her feel sleepy and dizzy, increased her weight, and blurred her vision. Some of the side effects passed after a few weeks. She takes another medication to deal with the others. Jennifer also must have frequent blood tests to check the level of lithium in her blood and make sure her kidneys and thyroid are working correctly. Too much lithium can damage a person's kidneys. Sometimes lithium interferes with the thyroid, and another medication is needed to treat the thyroid problem.

A person who undergoes ECT may not be able to remember the treatment or other events and may be confused for a half hour or so. Some people have headaches or sore muscles for a short time. Usually a patient's memory returns in a few weeks. In rare cases, people may lose the memory of important events in their lives forever. ECT also can trigger mania in some people. They may be given lithium or another mood stabilizer before having ECT.

Sometimes it takes people several months—in some cases, years—to find the treatment that works best for them. Lithium takes a few weeks to have an effect and as much as a year for the best results. A person taking anti-depressants may have to wait four weeks or more to feel better. Psychotherapy can go on for years. Usually, however, people can learn how to change behavior or how to alter ways of thinking over a three-to-six-month period. Often, benefits are seen as early as three to six weeks after treatment begins.

Even when they find a treatment that works, people may still have some shifts in mood. Sometimes medicines stop working, and the patients have to change the dose or switch to another medication.

"My Life Is Finally Back on Track"

Treatment can make a dramatic difference in the lives of those who suffer from depression or mania. For many, the beneficial change is worth the wait and the struggle to deal with side effects. "Life is much easier," said Jennifer Ellis, since she began treatment. "Medications helped me look at life in a stable way. I feel my life is finally back on track and I'm ready to go."

Erin's father realized what a difference Erin's treatment

had made when he came home from work grouchy and upset after a hard day. In the past her father's mood would have triggered an angry outburst from Erin. Instead she calmly told her father, "Daddy, I can tell you've had a bad day. I hope you feel better, because it's upsetting to me."

Since undergoing treatment, Erin said she has more friends at school and she avoids fights with her parents and brothers. The medication helps to keep her calm, and the therapy teaches her how to behave suitably. "I can tell it's working," she said. "Now I can be a kid again."

Her mother says the change in Erin has been remarkable. "She would have a temper tantrum and run away in the middle of the winter with no shoes or coat on. It was scary. Now little things no longer set her off. I've got my daughter back."

For Jim Boisvert, now twenty-one, getting treatment has affected everything in his life, "from the time I wake up in the morning to the time I go to bed at night." Now working full-time, he is saving money to get his own apartment or go to college. He has given up drugs and alcohol, which he began abusing when he was in junior high school. "I'm no longer gripped by sadness or gripped by madness," he said. He can control his life "as much as the next person, which is all I really ask. It's sort of comforting to know I won't have moods for no reason."

After Rachel began taking the antidepressant Zoloft, her depression lifted for the first time in years. "I felt I wasn't just coping," she said. "I finally experienced life without depression. I could think more sharply than I ever did in my life. I had more energy than ever before. Life was actually fun."

Chapter 6

Coping and Hope

Researchers continue to study the brain. They are trying to learn more about what causes mental illness and how to treat it. With that information they hope someday to prevent mental illness or to find a cure. Until then, however, people with mental disorders search for ways to deal with their illnesses, cope with side effects from their medication, and endure taunts and hurtful treatment from others.

Even though extensive research links mood disorders to a chemical imbalance, many people still think that those who have

Researchers continue to try to find a way to cure mental illness.

depression or bipolar disorder are to blame for their illness. According to the National Mental Health Association, 43 percent of those polled said they thought depression was a weakness in character rather than an illness. People with depression may be accused of being lazy or weak-willed. Friends and family members often think a child who is manic is simply misbehaving. They blame the parents for not raising their children "properly."

Some people fear those with mental illness or are prejudiced against them. Because of this, many people don't seek help for mental disorders. They are either ashamed to admit they may need medication or are afraid of the reaction of others if they admit they have a mental problem.

Rachel and Erin asked that their full names not be used in this book because they feared people would treat them badly if they knew they had mood disorders. Jennifer Ellis agreed to let her name be used, even though some students at her school called her "Psycho Lady" after her return from the treatment center. "It really hurt me," Jennifer recalled. "They don't know what my life has been like and how many times I've tried to get help." She spoke to the school's guidance counselor about the incident and got support from friends.

"Mental illness is not like a virus," Jennifer said. "It's not something you can avoid." She believes people need to know more about mental illness so they will be more understanding. Hoping someday to work as a counselor at a treatment center for people who are mentally ill, Jennifer says, "I'd like to help people."

Jennifer has a list of steps she hopes will guide others who have mood disorders:

- Find the right medication.
- Take deep breaths and try to calm down.
- Identify the stressful things that make you manic (or depressed).
- Talk with a therapist.
- Take one thing at a time, and do it at your own pace.
- Express your feelings to someone who will support you.
- Stay around positive people.
- Seek out support systems.
- Help yourself.

John Boisvert, 18, says the support of his family has helped him cope with bipolar disorder.

Jim Boisvert's brother, John, who also has bipolar disorder, said the support of his family and his own will to keep going get him through the bad times. "It's not an easy thing to overcome," he said.

Rachel adds her own words of advice: "Learn as much as you can about your illness. Don't be ashamed of taking medication. Know that the mood can lift."

Perhaps the most important thing to remember, she said, is that there's hope.

Further Reading

Clayton, Lawrence, and Sharon Carter. *Coping with Depression*. Sherman Oaks, Calif.: Hazelden Foundation, 1997.

Garland, E. Jane. *Depression Is the Pits, but I'm Getting Better: A Guide for Adolescents*. Washington, D.C.: American Psychological Association, 1998.

Hyde, Margaret O., and Elizabeth H. Forsyth, M.D. *Know About Mental Illness*. New York: Walker & Co., 1996.

———. *The Violent Mind*. Danbury, Conn.: Franklin Watts, 1991.

Jaffe, Steven L. *Prozac and Other Antidepressants*. New York: Chelsea House, 1999.

Jamison, Kay. *An Unquiet Mind: A Memoir of Moods and Madness*. New York: Random House, Inc., 1995.

Johnson, Julie T. *Understanding Mental Illness: For Teens Who Care About Someone with Mental Illness*. Minneapolis: Lerner Publishing Group, 1990.

Sherrow, Victoria. *Mental Illness*. San Diego: Lucent Books, 1995.

Silverstein, Dr. Alvin, Virginia Silverstein, and Laura S. Nunn. *Depression*. Springfield, N.J.: Enslow Publishers, 1997.

Stewart, Gail B. *Teens & Depression*. San Diego: Lucent Books, 1997.

For More Information

The following is a list of organizations and Internet resources that deal with bipolar disorder and depression.

Organizations

American Academy of Child and Adolescent Psychiatry
3615 Wisconsin Ave., N.W., Washington, D.C. 20016-3007; (202) 966-7300; <http://www.aacap.org>

American Psychiatric Association
1400 K St., N.W., Suite 1101, Washington, D.C. 20005-2403; (202) 682-6000, (888) 267-5400; <http://www.psych.org>

American Psychological Association
750 First St., N.E., Washington, D.C. 20002; (202) 336-5500; <http://www.apa.org>

Disability Rights Education and Defense Fund
(DREDF), 2212 Sixth St., Berkeley, CA 94710; (800) 466-4232; <http://www.dredf.org>

National Alliance for the Mentally Ill
2107 Wilson Blvd., Suite 300, Arlington, VA 22201-3042; (703)524-7600, (800) 950-NAMI (6264); <http://www.nami.org>

National Depressive and Manic-Depressive Association
730 N. Franklin, #501, Chicago, IL 60610; (800) 82N-DMDA (826-3632); <http://www.ndmda.org>

National Foundation for Depressive Illness, Inc.
P.O. Box 2257, New York, NY 10116; (800) 239-1265;
<http://www.depression.org>

National Institute of Mental Health
6001 Executive Blvd., Rm. 8184, MSC 9663,
Bethesda, MD 20892-9663; (301) 43-4513;
<http://www.nimh.nih.gov>

National Mental Health Association
1021 Prince St., Alexandria, VA 22314-2971;
(800) 969-NMHA

National Mental Health Consumers Association
Self-Help Clearinghouse
1211 Chestnut St., Suite 1207, Philadelphia, PA
19107; (800) 553-4539

Internet Resources

<http://www.appi.org>
Maintained by the American Psychiatric Press, Inc.
<http://www.mhsource.com/bipolar/>
Online resources for people with bipolar disorder.
Links to other sites, list of books, information, and
links to support groups. Maintained by the Bipolar
Disorders Information Center.

Glossary

antidepressants—Medications used to treat depression that lift a patient's mood.

antiseizure medications—Medications used to prevent seizures; also used to treat bipolar disorder.

attention deficit hyperactivity disorder—A condition in which the brain doesn't focus as it should, making it hard for a person with the disorder to pay attention.

atypical depression—A form of unipolar depression (*see below*) in which people eat and sleep too much and feel as if their arms and legs are very heavy.

bipolar disorder—A mood disorder in which a person's moods shift from high to low (depression).

Bipolar I—A form of bipolar disorder in which a person shifts from very high moods to very low moods.

Bipolar II—A form of bipolar disorder similar to Bipolar I except that the high moods are less severe (hypomanic).

chronic illnesses—Illnesses that last a long time, usually for the life of the patient.

cyclothymic disorder—A mild form of bipolar disorder with high and low moods that are less extreme.

delusions of grandeur—Unrealistic beliefs that a person can do the impossible or is someone famous.

depression—A feeling of despair; the "low" of bipolar disorder. *See also* unipolar depression.

dopamine—A neurotransmitter that helps a person focus or pay attention; it also can make a person feel high.

dysthymia—A mild form of depression in which a person feels sad almost all the time for years at a time.

electroconvulsive therapy (ECT)—A treatment used for mood disorders in which a small electrical current is passed through the brain, causing a seizure.

epinephrine—A neurotransmitter that raises the blood pressure and speeds up the heart, enabling a person to respond quickly to an emergency.

flight of ideas—A manic state in which a person's thoughts or speech switches rapidly from one thing to another, so quickly that others often cannot follow what is being said.

genes—Tiny units within the body cells that determine a person's features.

hallucinate—To hear voices or see images that aren't there.

hypomanic—Having a mild form of mania, feeling very happy.

lithium—A medication used to treat bipolar disorder, which lessens mood swings.

mania—A feeling of great happiness; a high.

manic depression—*See* bipolar disorder.

melancholic depression—*See* typical depression.

mixed bipolar disorder—A form of bipolar disorder in which a person feels symptoms of both mania and depression at the same time.

monoamine oxidase inhibitors (MAOIs)—Medications used to treat depression and other mood disorders; can't be mixed with certain foods or medications.

mood disorder—A mental illness affecting a person's mood.

neurons—A nerve cell that carries messages back and forth between parts of the body and the brain.

neurotransmitter—A chemical that transmits messages along the neurons between the brain and other parts of the body.

norepinephrine—A neurotransmitter linked to happiness and sadness.

paranoid delusions—Unrealistic fears that others may hurt or kill the fearful person.

psychotherapy—Treatment of mental disorders in which a person discusses his or her problems with a therapist.

psychotic—Having lost touch with reality.

rapid cyclers—People who shift rapidly between mania and depression, at least four times a year.

schizophrenia—A form of mental illness in which a person no longer knows what is real; may include delusions and hallucinations.

seasonal affective disorder—A condition that affects people in fall and winter when there is less sunlight; symptoms include depression, listlessness, irritability, and overeating.

selective serotonin reuptake inhibitors (SSRIs)—Antidepressants used to treat depression and other mood disorders.

serotonin—A neurotransmitter in the brain that has been linked to sleep and emotions.

side effects—Usually unpleasant symptoms caused by a medication or treatment.

symptoms—Signs of disease or behavior caused by a disease or disorder; for example, a deep sadness that lasts for a long time may be a symptom of depression.

therapist—A person trained to deal with mental problems.

thought racing—A manic state in which ideas race through a person's head.

tranquilizers—Medications used to calm people.

typical depression—A form of unipolar depression in which a person feels tired, can't sleep, eats too little, and has no interest in life.

unipolar depression—A mood disorder in which a person feels sad most of the time. Often referred to as simply depression.

Index

AA Z-2608